T0071003

SongStream

10 Songs for Youth Choirs

Compiled and Edited by

Bob Chilcott & Peter Hunt

MUSIC DEPARTMENT

OXFORD
UNIVERSITY PRESS

OXFORD
UNIVERSITY PRESS

Great Clarendon Street, Oxford OX2 6DP, England
198 Madison Avenue, New York, NY10016, USA

Oxford University Press is a department of the University of Oxford.
It furthers the University's aim of excellence in research, scholarship,
and education by publishing worldwide

Oxford is a registered trade mark of Oxford University Press
in the UK and in certain other countries

© Oxford University Press 2005

The various composers have asserted their right under the Copyright, Designs
and Patents Act, 1988, to be identified as the Composers of this Work.

Database right Oxford University Press (maker)

First published 2005

All rights reserved. No part of this publication may be reproduced,
stored in a retrieval system, or transmitted, in any form or by any means,
without the prior permission in writing of Oxford University Press,
or as expressly permitted by law. Enquiries concerning reproduction
outside the scope of the above should be sent to the Music Copyright
Department, Oxford University Press, at the address above

Permission to perform the works in this anthology in public
(except in the course of divine worship) should normally be obtained
from the Performing Right Society Ltd. (PRS), 29/33 Berners Street,
London W1T 3AB, or its affiliated Societies in each country throughout
the world, unless the owner or the occupier of the premises
being used holds a licence from the Society

Permission to make a recording must be obtained in advance
from the Mechanical Copyright Protection Society Ltd. (MCPS),
Elgar House, 41 Streatham High Road, London SW16 1ER,
or its affiliated Societies in each country throughout the world

12

ISBN 0-19-343545-4 978-0-19-343545-2

Music and text origination by
Barnes Music Engraving Ltd., East Sussex
Printed in Great Britain on acid-free paper by
Halstan & Co. Ltd., Amersham, Bucks.

Contents

4

Performance Notes
by Bob Chilcott & Peter Hunt

1. Aka-Tonbo
This beautiful pentatonic melody was sung to me by a husky-voiced Japanese lady in London in 1983. I arranged it for the vocal group The Light Blues for a tour of Japan, subsequently reworked it for the BBC Singers in 2005, and then made this version a little later. The melody needs to flow simply and naturally, and be shaped to follow its rise and fall. The accompaniment should be sustained and unforced; stagger the breathing in the hummed sections to provide an unbroken backdrop to the melody.

An English prose translation is:
The red dragonflies fly at sunset. When I was young, and riding on nanny's back, I saw them. We picked mulberry fruits into a little basket in the field of a mountain. Or was it just a dream? At fifteen she married and was gone. Letters never seemed to come.
The red dragonflies fly at sunset. Look, one now rests on a bamboo stick.

2. Blue Mountain river
This original melody by folk singer Cara Dillon should be sung as naturally as possible, in a *legato* style, and supported by a good breath before each phrase. Singers will need to practise really clean unison singing, with vowels and tone that match. The words depict the river as a source of comfort, consolation, and inspiration; make these clear but not overdone so they don't break up the musical phrases. Aim for a warm and gently passionate sound, with a gentle and sustained piano accompaniment. Verse 4 should have more energy in the vocal tone and a strong piano climax in bars 37–8. A solo voice could sing the start of verse 5 up to the end of bar 46 to create more variety of texture.

3. Can you hear me?
I originally wrote this piece in 1998 for a children's choir festival at DisneyWorld in Florida. I never intended the song to be sentimental, rather to be robust and positive. The signing suggested here is only a skeleton suggestion—perhaps someone in your community who knows sign language can help. I like it best when the whole choir signs—when the hands of the singers look like they are dancing, or like flocks of birds.

4. Give me strength
This song is taken from *Circlesong*, a large-scale work for SAB choir, SATB choir, two pianos and percussion. The words are Native American, and present the story and cycle of life. This song comes from the section that portrays youth, and the text asks for the strength to go out into the world. It needs to be sung positively and with conviction; singers should sing through the long notes in the tune and feel the steady pulse of the music moving the song forward.

5. How can I keep from singing?
This is another strong traditional tune that flows well. Start by practising the rising four-note motif (bar 2), checking for accurate tuning and vocal blend across the choir. The words are ever-hopeful: whether surrounded by pain or joy, you can't stop yourself singing, so keep that atmosphere with a bright smile to the sound. Aim for a firm tone that keeps its energy to the ends of phrases, particularly those that end with a rising interval, such as bars 23 and 31. The song builds in intensity to verse 3 (bar 55) which is sung in

canon, entering at the * sign. This works well in four or six equal parts, though more are possible. It can be made more urgent (as suggested by the words) if the voices enter at (*) instead. At the end of the canon voices should repeat the final phrase 'from singing?' until all parts have joined together. The effect should be a busy and tumultuous sound above a strong piano part which loops the repeated bars at the bottom of page 36.

6. The Ribbon
The poet John Mole has written the words specially for this song, the first of a set of four songs called *Messages in a Bottle*. I imagine this song to be sung almost like a pop song, delivered simply and with echoes of James Taylor. Make sure the chords are well balanced and that the rhythms and syncopations are clean. Work towards a warm *forte* at bar 13, before subsiding to the gentle dynamic of the opening.

7. Shake the bottle
The text of this second song from *Messages in a Bottle* encourages us to celebrate the joy of life here and now. The vocal lines need to be sung with much energy and crisp syncopations—make sure these are confident and together. All the descant soprano parts are optional, and the percussion parts can be played *ad lib.*, with as few or as many instruments as you like.

8. Swing low, sweet chariot
This well-known spiritual is here given up-tempo and energetic treatment. Singing should be very rhythmic and full of conviction, with clear words and strong consonants placed right at the front of the mouth. Take a moment to sort out the order of singing. The first chorus is sung in unison, baritones add their line the second time, while sopranos sing their top line third and fourth times (altos on the melody throughout). The order of the verses is: verse 1 baritones, verse 2 altos, verse 3 sopranos, with everyone singing 'Comin' for to carry me home' in unison each time. The harmony in bars 29–30 needs to be strong and joyous, leading back to the chorus. The Coda should feel quietly intense, building to a huge shout of 'HOME!' at the end.

9. Three country dances in one
In this spirited round, Thomas Ravenscroft, the first known publisher of folksongs in England, puts together three dances, in soprano, alto, and tenor, each one having plain and direct words on different subjects. He then adds a bass part which announces what is happening in the piece! The singing style should be light, with bouncing energy and a one-in-a-bar feel to the rhythm with weight on the first beat. A performance should begin with each group (or a solo) singing through their dance first, before building them up in the suggested order (BTAS). It is possible to perform this piece with all upper voices (SSAA), or all changed voices (TTBarB), in the key that suits best the voice ranges.

10. With a little help from my friends
This well-known song is intended here to be sung slightly faster than the Beatles' original. Verse 1 is unison, and the baritones sing their line for verses 2 and 3. The tune is syncopated throughout, so make sure the backing vocals are clearly on the beat with straight rhythm as written; practise them separately. The chorus words need a lot of light articulation, particularly 'with a little help from my friends'. The Tag can be used in a variety of ways as suggested on page 64; it could also be used as an introduction, building up each line at a time, with or without audience participation.

for Michael Kibblewhite and the Cantate Youth Choir

1. Aka-Tonbo

Rofuu Miki
(1889-1964)

KOSAKU YAMADA
(1886-1965)

arr. BOB CHILCOTT

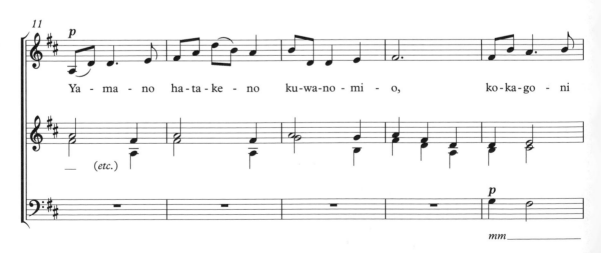

© Oxford University Press 2005 and 2006. Photocopying this copyright material is ILLEGAL.

Yu - ya - ke ko-ya-ke - no a-ka-to - n - bo, to-ma - te i - ru - yo

mm _____ mm _____

(etc.)

(etc.)

sa-o-no - sa - ki. mm _____

mm _____

mm ____

mm ____

2. Blue Mountain river

additional lyrics Peter Hunt

Words and music
CARA DILLON and **SAM LAKEMAN**
arr. **PETER HUNT**

© 2000 & 2005 Rough Trade Music Ltd & EMI Music Publishing Ltd. Reproduced by permission of International Music Publications Ltd for Europe, EMI Music Publishing Ltd for Australia, New Zealand, & South East Asia, & EMI Blackwood Music Inc for the USA & Canada. All Rights Reserved. Photocopying this copyright material is ILLEGAL.

while. Hold my hand in dark-ness, when co-lours fade and die. I

feel you here be-side___ me, and I'm cap-tured by___ your tide.___ The

time will soon be o-ver___ and light be-gin to shine.

SOPRANOS
a tempo

5. Blue Moun - tain ri - ver___ I went there for a while. I
li - stened for an an - swer and I found it deep in - side. When I'm
lost be - hind the sha - dows, and I want to run___ and hide,___ my

Blue Moun-tain ri-ver____ is there right by my side.

Blue Moun-tain ri-ver is there right by my side.

Blue Moun-tain ri-ver is there right by my side.

Blue Moun-tain ri-ver.____

Blue Moun-tain ri-ver.____

Blue Moun-tain ri-ver.____

Commissioned by Keynote Arts Associates – James E. Dash, President – for the Children in Harmony Choral Festival, Orlando, Florida, May 1998, Barbara Tagg, Artistic Director

3. Can you hear me?

Words and music
BOB CHILCOTT

This piece is also available in an orchestration for string orchestra and piano, available from the publisher's hire library.

© Oxford University Press 1998 and 2005. Photocopying this copyright material is ILLEGAL.

END SIGNING

mf espress.

too? My world's a si-lent one, but it's e - nough for me, I

hear you through your hands, the move-ment sets me free, but

it could be a spe-cial thing to hear your voice, to hear you sing.

it could be a spe-cial thing to hear you sing.

a tempo
SIGN
p Can___ you hear me?___
div.
pp Can you hear me?
unis.
Can___ you hear me
p
Can___ you hear me?___
p sempre
too?
Can___ you hear me?___
Can you hear me?
Can you hear me
p sempre
unis.
END SIGNING
too?
p
I look a-round me as I grow, I'd
mp espress.
dim.
like to tell you all I know.___
SIGN
rit.
slower
Can you hear___ me?
pp

Composer's Note

I wrote this piece to include sign language, as I have always found it to be an incredibly sensitive and beautiful form of communication—it also served as a reminder to me always to try to be open and aware of other people, and also of our surroundings. The three short choruses can be signed where marked.

BOB CHILCOTT

A GLOSSARY OF SIGN LANGUAGE *

British		American
	Can	
	You	
	See	
	Feel	
	Hear	
	Me	
	It (the sun)	(tap against head twice)
	Too	

* This glossary is for guidance only and choirs are encouraged to enlist the help of a fluent signer if it is possible.

to City of Birmingham Young Voices with David Lawrence,
and Birmingham Festival Choral Society with Jeremy Patterson

4. Give me strength

Sioux trad.

BOB CHILCOTT

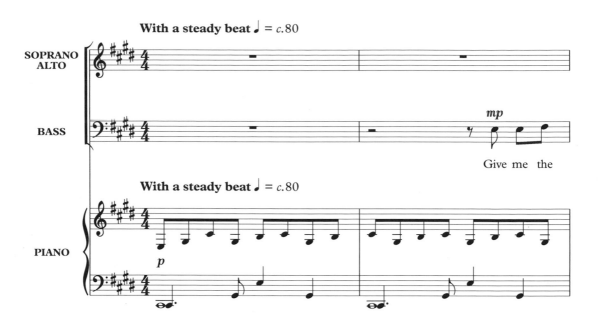

'Give me strength' is from the cantata *Circlesong*, a 'Life Cycle' based on Native American writings for SAB choir, SATB choir, two pianos and percussion (available for hire from the publishers).

© Oxford University Press 2003 and 2005. Photocopying this copyright material is ILLEGAL.

a few **SOPRANOS**

Look u-pon, u-pon these fa - ces___

Look u - pon these fa - ces_____ of

_ of chil - dren with-out num-ber and with

chil - dren with - out num-ber___ and with

chil - dren in their arms._____ With your power on - ly can they face the

chil - dren in their arms._____ With your power on - ly can they face the

winds and walk the good road_ to the day_ of quiet.

winds and walk the good road_ to the day_ of quiet. With your

5. How can I keep from singing?

Traditional
additional lyrics Peter Hunt

?ROBERT LOWRY
arr. PETER HUNT

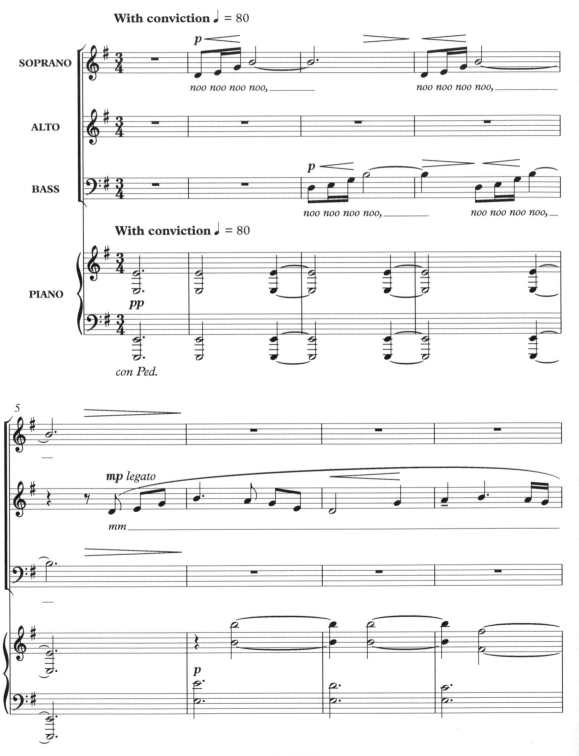

© Oxford University Press 2005. Photocopying this copyright material is ILLEGAL.

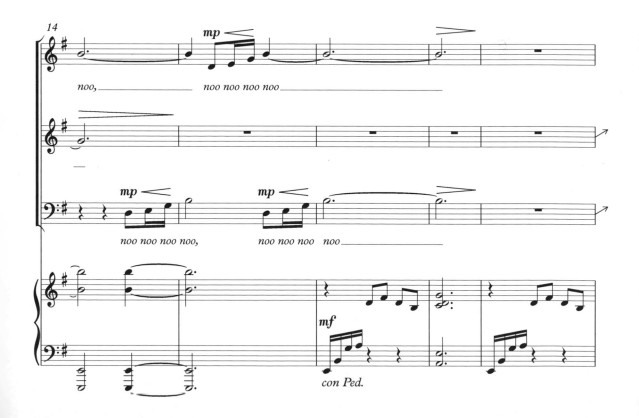

1. My life goes on in end-less song, a - bove earth's la-men-ta-tion; I hear the

real though far-off call hail-ing a bright and new cre - a-tion. Through all the tur - moil

and the strife, I hear its mu-sic ring-ing. It sounds an e - cho in my soul; how can I

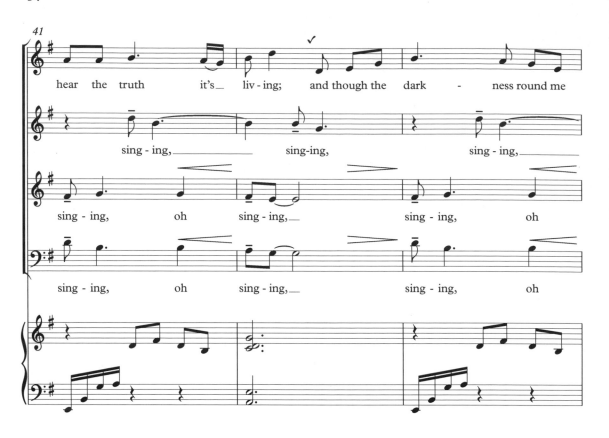

hear the truth it's— liv-ing; and though the dark - ness round me

sing - ing,_____ sing-ing, sing - ing,_____

sing - ing, oh sing - ing,__ sing - ing, oh

sing - ing, oh sing - ing,__ sing - ing, oh

folds, songs in the night it's gi - ving. No storm can

__ sing-ing, how can I keep from sing - ing?__

sing-ing, oh sing - - ing. No storm can

sing - ing,__ how can I keep from sing - ing?__

for Michael Kibblewhite and the Cantate Youth Choir

6. The Ribbon

(Messages in a Bottle, No. 1)

John Mole

BOB CHILCOTT

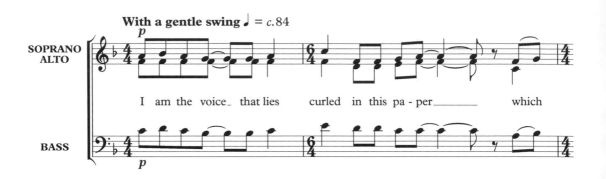

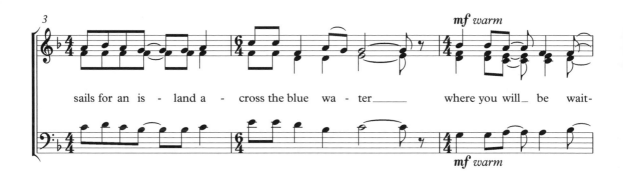

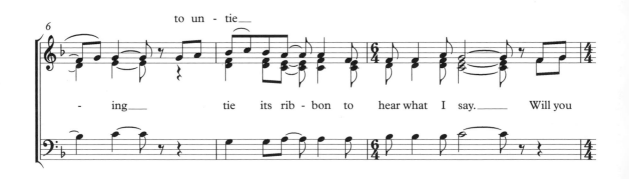

Text © John Mole 2005, used by permission. All rights reserved. Music © Oxford University Press 2005.
Photocopying this copyright material is ILLEGAL.

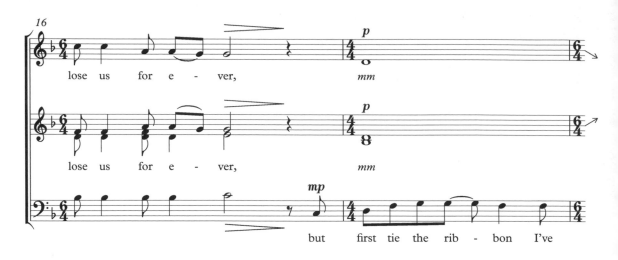

lose us for e - ver, *mm*

lose us for e - ver, *mm*

but first tie the rib - bon I've

*mm*_____ no not round a mes-sage,_____ *mm*_____

sent for your keep - ing,_____ but as I re-mem-ber it looped in your hair.

*mm*_____ *mm*_____

7. Shake the bottle

(*Messages in a Bottle*, No. 2)

John Mole

BOB CHILCOTT

Text © John Mole 2005, used by permission. All rights reserved. Music © Oxford University Press 2005.
Photocopying this copyright material is ILLEGAL.

Shake the bot - tle, pop the cork, cut the prat - tle, no___ more talk,___

Shake the bot - tle, pop the cork, cut the prat - tle, no___ more___

talk.

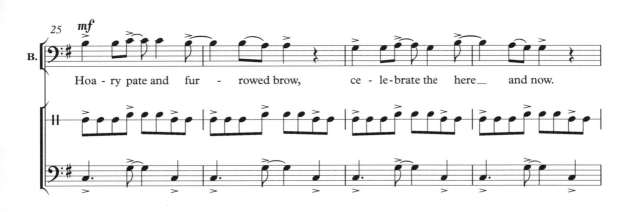

Hoa - ry pate and fur - rowed brow, ce - le-brate the here___ and now.

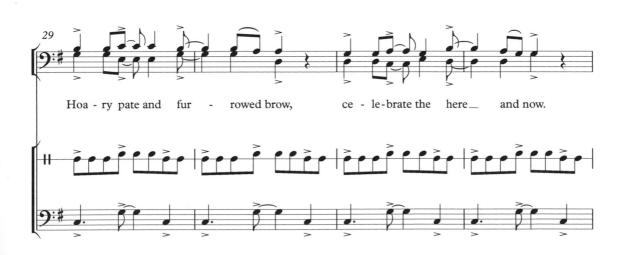

Hoa - ry pate and fur - rowed brow, ce - le-brate the here___ and now.

44

glas - ses, this the mes - sage as time pas - - ses!

this the mes - sage

DESCANT SOPRANOS (opt.)

Shake the bot - tle, pop the cork, cut the prat - tle, no___ more talk,___

Shake the bot - tle, pop the cork, cut the prat - tle, no___ more talk,___

Shake the bot-tle, pop the cork, cut the prat-tle, no___ more talk.

Shake the bot-tle, pop the cork, cut the prat-tle, no___ more talk.

Young or old don't waste_ a_ min-ute, yours is the world and all___ that's in it.

Young or old don't waste_ a_ min - ute, yours is the world and all___ that's in it.

DESCANT SOPRANOS (opt.)

Shake the bot - tle, pop the cork, cut the prat-tle, no___ more talk,___

Shake the bot - tle, pop the cork, cut the prat-tle, no___ more talk,___

Shake the bot-tle, pop the cork, cut the prat-tle, no____ more talk.

Shake the bot-tle, pop the cork, cut the prat-tle, no____ more talk.

shake the bot-tle, shake the bot-tle, no____ more talk.

shake the bot-tle, shake the bot-tle, no____ more talk.

8. Swing low, sweet chariot

Spiritual
arr. **PETER HUNT**

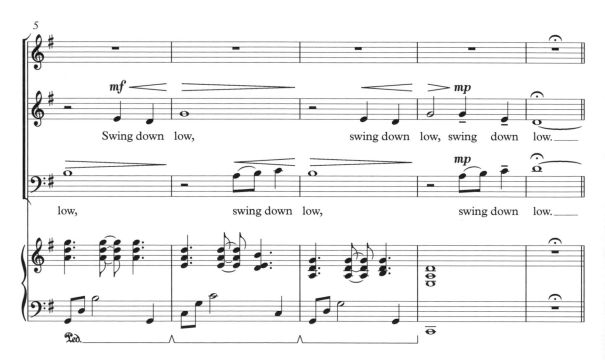

© Oxford University Press 2005. Photocopying this copyright material is ILLEGAL.

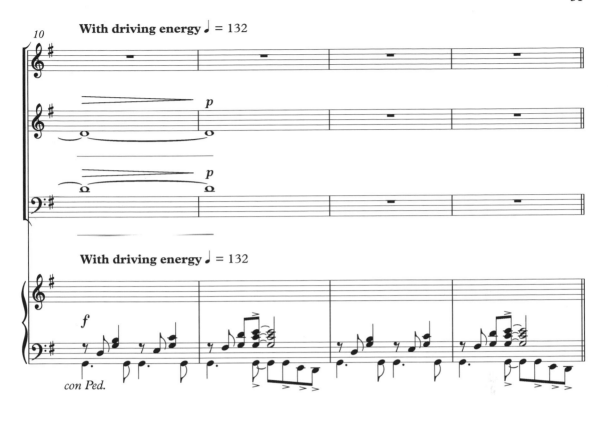

CODA

Car-ry me home,_____ car-ry me home,_____

Car-ry me home,_____ car-ry me home,_____

Car-ry me home,_____ car-ry me home,_____

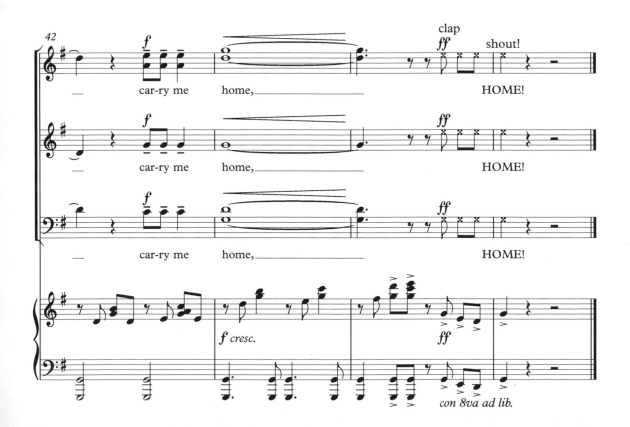

___ car-ry me home,_____ HOME!

___ car-ry me home,_____ HOME!

___ car-ry me home,_____ HOME!

9. Three country dances in one
(A round)

THOMAS RAVENSCROFT
(*c.*1582–*c.*1635)

BASS

Sing af - ter fel - lows as you hear me, a toy that sel - dom is seen - a. Three coun - try dan - ces in one to be, a pret - ty con - ceit as I ween - a.

TENOR

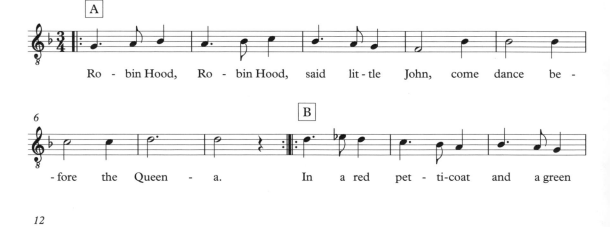

Ro - bin Hood, Ro - bin Hood, said lit - tle John, come dance be - fore the Queen - a. In a red pet - ti-coat and a green jack - et, a white hose and a___ green - a.

weena think

© Oxford University Press 2005. Photocopying this copyright material is ILLEGAL.

ALTO

The cramp is in my purse full_ sore, no mon - ey will bide there - in - a. Hey ho, the cramp - a, Hey ho, the cramp - a, Hey ho, the cramp - a, the cramp - a. The - a.

SOPRANO

Now foot it as I do_ Tom boy Tom, now foot it as I do Swith - en - a. And Hick thou must trick it all a - lone, till Ro - bin come leap - ing in be - tween - a.

The cramp is in my purse full sore a lack of money
foot it dance *Swithen* one of the dancers (a person's name) *trick it* dance

10. With a little help from my friends

Words and music
JOHN LENNON and **PAUL McCARTNEY**
arr. **PETER HUNT**

verse 1: unison throughout

f 1. What would you think if I sang out of tune, would you stand
mf 2. What do I do when my love is a-way, does it wor -
f 3. Would you be-lieve in a love at first sight? Yes I'm cer -

(verses 2 & 3 only)

We need friends;

con Ped.

© 1967 & 2005 Northern Songs / Sony/ATV Songs LLC. Used by permission of Music Sales Ltd & Sony/ATV Music Publishing.
All Rights Reserved. International Copyright Secured. Photocopying this copyright material is ILLEGAL.

_ up and walk_ out on me?_
- ry you to be_ a - lone?_
- tain that it hap-pens all the time._

Lend me your ears_ and I'll sing_
How do I feel_ by the end_
What do you see_ when you turn_

we   need   friends.   We   need

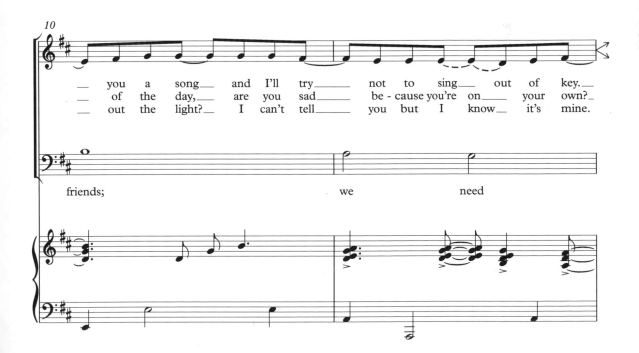

_ you a song_ and I'll try_ not to sing_ out of key._
_ of the day,_ are you sad_ be - cause you're on_ your own?_
_ out the light?_ I can't tell_ you but I know_ it's mine.

friends;   we   need

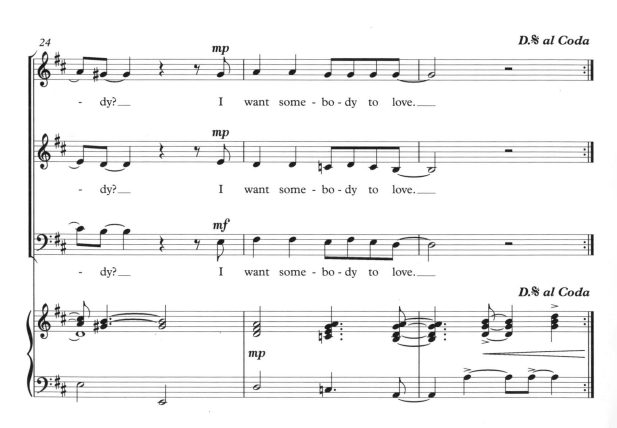

Tag

Tag

- The tag can be sung as a warm–up exercise to establish the tempo, style, and good ensemble before learning the piece.

- It can be taught orally, one part at a time, starting with soprano 1, then 2; alto then baritone. Once confident, a range of singing styles and dynamics can be explored.

- Off-beat handclaps will help to loosen the sound and create the right groove.

- The tag is effective when added in performance. After the coda, go straight to the tag without a break, and repeat it many times. It sounds good unaccompanied; singers can improvise around it and the audience can join in. If there are instruments playing they could improvise and let themselves go in some solo breaks.

- At an agreed signal the piano/instruments pick up the introduction, the singers stop on the word 'friends', and the whole song is sung again.